Leyland
Buses in
Camera

*The 'Gearless Bus' legend shows up clearly
on this 1937 Tiger TS8c with Craven 32-seat
body in the Sheffield Corporation fleet.*
G. H. F. Atkins

An impressive line of ten Tiger TS1 from the
Alexanders fleet seen in Dundee early in their
lives. They were new in 1929 and featured
Alexander 32-seat coach bodies.

Leyland

Buses in Camera

GAVIN BOOTH

IA

LONDON

IAN ALLAN LTD

First published 1981

ISBN 0 7110 1149 4

Published by Ian Allan Ltd, Shepperton, Surrey;
and printed by Ian Allan Printing Ltd at their works
at Coombelands in Runnymede, England

Jacket photo: *Fifty years of Leyland progress
is represented in this photograph taken at the
launch of the new Titan model in 1977. The
distinctive lines of the new bus compare with
the classic radiator of a preserved 1929
Titan TD1.* Gavin Booth

*Manchester Corporation favoured the
exposed-radiator Titan variants, like this
1958 PD2/40 with 65-seat body built by
Burlingham, a firm more readily identified
with single-deck coach bodywork at that
time. It is seen in Cheadle.* Leyland

Contents

Acknowledgements
My thanks are due to a number of people who have helped me in the preparation of this book. Firstly to the photographers, who are credited on these pages; many of them supplied large and excellent selections of photographs, and this made the final choice more difficult. Jasper Pettie helped with caption information, and Stewart Brown read through the final manuscript. And I must record my grateful thanks to the many Leyland officials who have assisted me by supplying photographs and information over a number of years.

A policeman obligingly holds back a 1933 oil-engined Titan TD3 of Leicester Corporation, with Metro-Cammell 56-seat bodywork. The TD3 introduced the squarer style of Leyland radiator which remained familiar until the war stopped production. Leyland

Introduction

A classic Leyland of the 1930s, a Tiger TS7 with stylish Duple coachwork.

The fact that a small workshop producing steam lawnmowers grew to become the heart of Britain's indigenous car industry could never have been prophesied in 1896 when James Sumner and Henry Spurrier set up in business as the Lancashire Steam Motor Co Ltd in the village of Leyland, near Preston. As recently as 1960 it was unthinkable that the structure of the British car and commercial vehicle industry would change as much as it subsequently did, and Leyland must have seemed an unlikely foundation on which to build.

Yet with the formation of the British Leyland Motor Corporation in 1968, many once-competitive firms found themselves strange bedfellows. The problems of BLMC, moulding together totally different philosophies, has been well-documented, and most comedians have a repertoire of jokes about the ouput of British Leyland car workers.

So the Leyland name that was once familiar mainly to bus and lorry men, and observant passengers, suddenly passed into the national vocabulary — even if its use was not always complimentary.

Today the Leyland name appears on a wide variety of buses, and it would take a whole series of these *Buses in Camera* books to do them justice. So this book is only concerned with what the purists might call 'real' Leylands — those designed and built at Leyland, Lancs, and not at Bathgate, Scotstoun, Southall or Wolverhampton; nor indeed those Fleetlines built at (and named after) Leyland. Leyland Leylands, in fact — for many other 'Leylands' have been, or will be, covered in separate books in the series.

The only non-Leyland, Lancs, buses which I have included are the Kingston-upon-Thames Cubs of the 1930s, the recent integral Leylands, the National and Titan built at Workington, and the Olympian chassis, built at Bristol.

I have concentrated on home-market Leylands, in the interests of available space. Right from the early days, Leyland's export activities have been a significant part of the business, but to ensure a fair coverage of Leyland's home-market bus sales only a token export selection could be included. The same must be true of Leyland's trolleybuses, produced in reasonable quantity in the decade leading to World War 2; here again space dictates that the book must concentrate on motor buses.

The course of the bus industry's relationship with Leyland has not always run smoothly, particularly in the troubled early years of BLMC, when so many things seemed to go wrong. But Leyland seems to have heeded its critics, and has gone about moulding its bus range to suit customer demand in a most impressive way. If we British are permitted a touch of chauvinism at a time when this appears to be unfashionable — and if we are honest — most of us are firmly behind Leyland Bus, and willing the company to succeed in a difficult market. The signs are certainly encouraging.

Gavin Booth Edinburgh

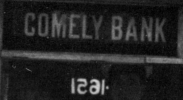

COMELY BANK

LEYLAND

SG-1651

A Haslingden-style Leyland X of around 1909, for the Metropolitan Asylum Board.

Progress from Lawnmowers

The Leyland story has been one of diversification and expansion. And this was the case right from the days of the Lancashire Steam Motor Co. Although the new company, set up in the small Lancashire town of Leyland in 1896, started building steam lawnmowers and wagons, by 1900 the first steam bus had been built, and by 1901 the firm had earned its first export order.

Although steam vehicles were produced for some years, many builders were turning to petrol engines, and in 1904 an experimental lorry was built at Leyland. A production petrol chassis soon went on the market, and in 1905 the company won an order for double-deck buses for the London & Suburban Omnibus Co, which with Leyland investment became the London Central company. The company built up a large Leyland fleet before selling out to London General in 1912. Other early Leyland bus customers included Birch Bros, and Manchester Corporation.

In 1907 a rival builder of steam vehicles, based in nearby Preston, was bought over and Lancashire Steam Motor Co was renamed Leyland Motors Ltd. In the same year two new petrol models were introduced, the X and U types, which were normal control chassis, suitable for goods or passenger work in the fashion of the time.

Over the years until the outbreak of war in 1914 Leyland's production of steam vehicles reduced while petrol vehicles increased greatly. At a time when there were many manufacturers competing for the business of the embryo bus industry, Leylands were chosen by many of the operators starting out in business; some of these operators survive today, and many still buy Leylands.

Some of these early Leyland buses had Leyland-built bodies. Few bus chassis manufacturers became involved in bodybuilding activities, and certainly none to the extent of Leyland's involvement over a span of some 40 years.

Then in 1912 the War Office held its subsidised vehicle trials to determine the types most suitable to qualify for a subsidy towards the purchase price and upkeep; the War Department could re-purchase the vehicles if required. A 3-ton Leyland was chosen, and many orders followed. In the event this was just as well, for the outbreak of war meant that these chassis *were* required — and the first mechanised war in history meant that large numbers of similar vehicles were needed. These were not buses, of course, but the chassis that became widely known as the RAF model was to be used for buses in peacetime.

Leyland's wartime production figures were impressive. In just over four years nearly 6,000 vehicles were produced for the War Office — compared with just over 2,000 petrol models in the previous decade.

The essential expansion during the war meant that Leyland was well placed in 1919 to cope with the return to normal production. But with thousands of RAF chassis surplus to WD requirements and likely to flood

The Edinburgh-type body, fitted, appropriately to a 1920 Edinburgh Corporation G7, here seen in 1922 fitted with pneumatic tyres.
Lothian Region Transport

the market, Leyland set about re-purchasing and reconditioning them. In fact, more than 3,000 passed through a former aircraft factory at Kingston-upon-Thames. Most were resold for further use and many became buses, but what was an admirable action to protect the company's reputation turned out to be unsound in time of financial stringency.

Production of bus models at Leyland re-started with a wide range of chassis to suit different needs. Many of these carried Leyland bodies, initially the open charabanc styles of the time, and then saloon and double-deck bodies. Most buses and lorries at the time were of the normal control layout, with the driver behind the engine. Leyland also experimented with over-type vehicles, with the driver perched on top of the engine, but forward control, dubbed 'side-type' by Leyland quickly caught on.

The most popular bus chassis of the time was the G series, particularly the G7 and its forward control equivalent the SG7.

Leyland had been unable to penetrate the lucrative London bus market since its early successes with the London Central company. The London General Omnibus Company had built its own chassis since 1909, and since 1912 these had borne the initials of another Underground subsidiary, Associated Equipment Company, AEC. With an in-house supply of buses and a virtual monopoly of the London bus services, AECs were all-powerful, and the LGOC had no need for Leyland chassis. In 1922 that monopoly was threatened by competition, and the pioneering 'pirate' Chocolate Express company used Leylands, as did many of the other independents which swarmed on to the London streets over the next few years. The Leylands used were LB models, similar to the G7, but built to a lighter specification to suit the Metropolitan Police requirements.

Some LB chassis were bought by provincial operators, but double-deckers were still far from common outside London. Otherwise, the Leyland bus range continued to be varied, solid and reliable. But the bus business was changing and the expanding industry was demanding more sophisticated, more suitable vehicles. Several builders were working on a new breed of pneumatic-tyred bus chassis. Leyland's contribution burst on to the scene in 1925, and really marked the emergence of Leyland as a responsible, front-line manufacturer.

A 1905 advertisement for the Lancashire Steam Motor Co Ltd, showing one of the six double-deck models supplied that year to the London & Suburban Omnibus Company. The Leyland name was still to come to the fore, and was used mainly as a model name until Leyland Motors was formed in 1907.
Gavin Booth Collection

Haslingden Corporation's first motor bus was this 1906 X type with 18-seat bodywork also built by Leyland. It features the early style of radiator, with deep top tank carrying the maker's name on an oval badge.   Leyland

A tiered charabanc body with seats for 23 passengers, mounted on a 1906 X type chassis. Luggage space was provided under the raised floor, and side curtains were available in case of inclement weather. Leyland

Todmorden Corporation's 1907 U type was the first of an unbroken line of Leylands supplied to that operator over the years. The body layout was typical of most double-deckers built at that time, owing much to the designs evolved for horse buses.   Leyland

Typical of large numbers of charabancs built in the years before and after World War 1, these two 1919 Blackpool-registered Leyland N types feature a more familiar radiator shape, which survived in a recognisable form right through to the appearance of the last Titan in 1969. Leyland

A neat little B type, dating from around 1920, with simple, but functional, Leyland-built body, featuring the distinctive front unsweep in the waist moulding. It was supplied to the Glasgow operator Rankin Bros. Leyland

Another 1920 Scottish Leyland, an N type charabanc for MacDougall's, Oban. Leyland

A well-laden 1921 Leyland charabanc of the Maidstone & District company, one of the longest-established of today's large fleets. For many, charabancs offered the first opportunity to travel around Britain at a reasonable cost, and gave many passengers their first glimpse of the seaside.
Maidstone & District

The double-deck bus was still a comparative rarity outside London and the main British cities, and this G type of the early 1920s must have attracted much attention when it entered service in rural Cornwall, for Pioneer of Breage, near Helston. Leyland

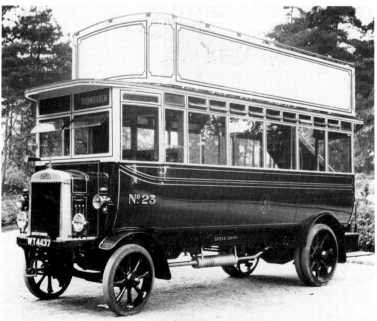

The giant Alexanders fleet in Scotland was an enthusiastic Leyland user, and the fleets of its present-day successors still include large numbers of Leyland products. This was one of the first Leylands in the Alexanders fleet, a 1923 SG7 with Crosville-type 40-seat body. Scottish Bus Group

Another early 'side-type' (forward control) Leyland, a 1923 SG4 for the Todmorden Corporation fleet. It had a 51-seat body, built by Leyland. Leyland

Leyland

The Roar of Lions and Tigers

Leyland's L range of 1925 was a clear step forward in bus design. For a start, here was a true bus chassis range, mostly forward control models, lower-built than the previous generation. There was the double-deck Leviathan, admittedly not a great success, with less than 100 chassis built. The Leopard was a rare single-deck chassis for 38-seat bodies, but its stablemate, the Lion, captured the orders. The Lion PLSC1 was the original model, and was joined by the longer PLSC3 in 1926, for bodies up to 26ft long. More than 2,500 Lions were built between 1925-1929, and its withdrawal from the model lists only followed the appearance of the improved LT chassis, in this time of rapid development.

The other L range models were the normal control Leveret and Lioness. The Leveret, designed for 20-seat bodies, was not a notable success; the imposing Lioness, for 26-seat bodies, was used for bus and coach work.

But if the 1925 L range, and the Lion in particular, helped put Leyland on the map, just two years later the appearance of the T type 6-cylinder engine and the legendary Tiger and Titan firmly cemented its position.

The new range introduced an advanced specification which was to set new standards in British bus design, popularising the concept of the 6-cylinder engine in a low-built chassis. The Tiger TS1 was the single-deck model, and had much in common with the double-deck Titan TD1, and while both models were immediately successful, the Titan created more of a sensation for it heralded the rebirth of the double-decker, finally closing the door on its horse bus origins. Outside London use of double-deck buses was still relatively limited, but the low build of the Titan, coupled with the lowbridge layout of the standard Leyland body, achieved a height of only 13ft, and this helped inspire confidence in a wide range of operators.

The Tiger TS2 joined the TS1 in 1928, a single-deck chassis with the same wheelbase, but intended for 26ft bodywork, rather than the 27ft 6in of the TS1. Then in 1929 these were joined by the TS3, with shorter wheelbase, again for 26ft bodies.

A third model was introduced in 1927, the six-wheel double-deck Titanic TT1 — an odd choice of name when you consider that the *Titanic* had sunk only 15 years before; and Leyland's Titanic was almost a disaster, with only six of the TT1 model built, while none of the subsequent TT2, TT3, TT4, TT5 and TT6 models could be called successful, particularly when compared with AEC's contemporary Renown six-wheelers.

But the two-axle Leylands continued their successful progress. The TD1 Titan appeared in Leyland-bodied highbridge form in 1929, and was succeeded by the TD2 in 1931, for slightly longer (26ft) bodies, and with a new 7.6litre engine replacing the original 6.8litre unit, triple servo brakes and fully-floating rear axles. At the same time the Tiger TS4 appeared, with the new engine, and in general the Titan and Tiger ranges moved forward in parallel during the 1930s, with successive models appearing together.

Leyland was not forgetting the market for middle-weight models, and the legendary PLSC3 Lion was replaced in 1929 by the LT1 Lion, sharing many parts with the Tiger, but with a 5.1litre 4-cylinder engine. The normal control Lioness PLC was replaced by the Lioness LTB1, which had the 6.8litre 6-cylinder engine. The LTB1 was offered until 1934, but demand for full-size bonneted chassis was limited. There was a continued market for the Lion range, however, and the improved LT2, LT3, and LT5 models appeared in 1930, 1931 and 1932.

The Leyland range still lacked lightweight models, and this omission was repaired in 1931 with the appearance of the normal control Cub range, built at the Kingston-upon-Thames factory, the original KP2 and KP3 models had a new 6-cylinder 4.4litre engine, and the 20-seat Cub found a market as a rural bus. Before long a forward control version, coded SKP, was offered, allowing up to 30-seat bodywork.

The frequent advances of the 1930s are reflected in the many changes to the Leyland model list. The most important change was the acceptance of the oil engine as standard for the vast majority of bus models. While other makers used proprietary makes of oil engine in their chassis, Leyland took time to develop its own range, culminating in the appearance of the famous 8.6litre unit in 1933. This engine was offered in the TD2 Titan and TS4 Tiger, although it was more familiar in the replacement TD3 and TS6 models, introduced in 1933.

Another development at the same time was the 'Gearless Bus', the name given to Leyland chassis fitted with the Lysholm-Smith hydraulic torque convertor, providing a certain amount of automatic gear control. This was available on the main heavier-weight chassis, and a TD3 Titan with torque converter was designated TD3c. Although available as an option throughout the 1930s, most operators stuck to the standard constant mesh gearbox; certainly it was never as successful as the Wilson preselective transmission adopted by Daimler and later by AEC.

The Lion range was updated with the LT5A in 1934, with a 4-cylinder 5.7litre diesel engine, and a new radiator which gave the model a more modern appearance. The Titan TD3 and Tiger TS6 had appeared with new-style radiators in 1933.

For the Alexanders fleet in Scotland, the LT5B Lion was offered in 1934, with the 8.6litre diesel engine of the Tiger. The LT6 of 1935 was a beefed-up LT5A for export.

. The Tiger range was itself developed by the introduction of the TS7 model in 1935, in petrol or diesel form, and with hydraulic brakes. The Titan and Lion ranges progressed at the same time with the TD4 and LT7 models.

There was still a limited market for six-wheel buses, and in addition to the Titanic double-decker, Leyland produced three-axle Tigers from 1934, coded TS6T, to signify the trailing third axle. Six-wheel TS7s were also built from 1935 — the TS7T and TS7D (with driven rear axle).

Leyland was primarily associated with full-sized, heavyweight bus chassis, but the smaller Cub range continued to sell in reasonable numbers, and was updated in 1935 with the KPZ and SKPZ models. The forward control SKP and SKPZ models revealed a demand for a larger lightweight model, and in 1935 this was met by the introduction of the Cheetah, a chassis of Lion dimensions and layout, but Cub mechanical components. The original Cheetah models were the LZ1 and LZ2, and when improved vacuum hydraulic brakes were fitted from 1936 the designations became LZ1A and LZ2A. The shorter LZ3 followed in 1937, and the LZ4 and LZ5 models replaced the existing models in 1938.

Leyland's customers in the 1930s were spread throughout Britain — and, indeed, the World. Most of the major British fleets bought Leylands, but the one notable exception was London Transport. Formed in 1933,

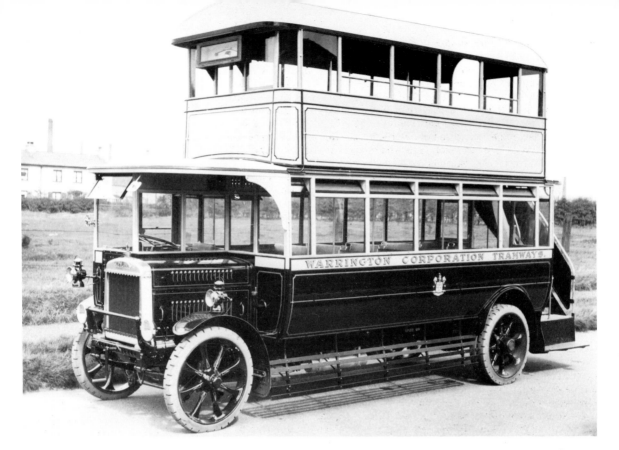

Introduced in 1925, the Leviathan double-deck chassis was not a great success. This LG1 model was built for Warrington Corporation in 1925, and was still mounted on solid tyres. The rather ungainly 55-seat body shows little real advance on the earliest double-deck motor buses, apart from the covered top.   Leyland

the giant London Passenger Transport Board succeeded London General as the principal bus operator in the Metropolis; London General had formed the Associated Equipment Company in 1912, primarily to build its chassis for London use, but while AEC did not pass to London Transport, AECs continued to dominate the London fleet. Leyland was anxious to break this near-monopoly, and in the 1930s successfully gained several orders, often for more specialised models. First were the 97 normal-control KPO3 Cubs supplied from 1934-36, and in 1936 there followed eight forward-control SKPZ2 Cubs, with $1\frac{1}{2}$-deck bodies for Inter-Station work.

More significant was the 1937 order for 100 Leyland double-deckers for London Transport, and these were TD4s with Leyland bodies — the last 10 were TD4c with torque converters. Leyland and London Transport continued to work together, and this resulted in the appearance of two interesting new single-deck models. First in 1937 was a prototype Tiger, with horizontal engine mounted under the floor, and a further 87 similar vehicles followed in 1939. Also in 1939/40 there appeared 49 rear-engined versions of the Cub, designed as a 20-seat one-man bus.

Leyland had been experimenting with different engine positions during the 1930s, and in 1936 had built a prototype rear-engined single-deck vehicle, but the London buses were the first rear-engined Leylands to enter service.

Development of the main ranges continued in 1937 with the appearance of the LT8 Lion, TS8 Tiger and TD5 Titan, which did not differ greatly from their predecessors. The LT9 Lion joined the LT8 in 1938.

Less conventional was the Gnu, a chassis with front-mounted engine, and twin-steering front axles; only buses with three axles could be 30ft long. Only eight Gnus, models TEP1 and TEC2, were built, in 1937 and 1939. One other six-wheel, twin-steer chassis was built, the Panda chassis of 1939 with an underfloor-mounted engine.

For Birmingham City Transport the Titan TD6c chassis was developed in 1938, and in 1939 the TD7 replaced the TD5 for other customers, with the TS11 its single-deck counterpart.

There was to have been a TD8 Titan, but the outbreak of war in 1939 prevented its introduction. Bus chassis production ceased in 1942, although some 200 Titans and Tigers were completed and released to operators that same year.

Leyland was first nominated as one of the builders of utility buses, but Leyland's resources were diverted instead to the production of military vehicles and armaments.

A 1928 Lion PLSC3 for Crosville, with Leyland 32-seat bodywork featuring front and rear doorways — the rear doorway being of the Scottish cutaway style. The body is also unusual as it lacks a roof-mounted destination indicator, further emphasising the pronounced dome shape.   Leyland

The classic lines of the Lion PLSC3 with Leyland bodywork. This 1927 example was new to Eastern Valleys, Pontypool, which became a Western Welsh subsidiary in 1929, being fully absorbed in 1932.

In Church Street, Athlone in the late 1920s, a 1928 Lion PLSC3 of the Great Southern Railways of Ireland.
Robert Grieves Collection

The short-lived Leveret normal-control model, represented here by an early LA2 example, with 20-seat Leyland body. With the withdrawal of the Leveret from the model lists in 1928, Leyland had no small-size bus chassis to offer until the appearance of the Cub in 1931.   Leyland

The stylish and imposing Lioness PLC1, Crosville 34 was one of nine 29-seat coaches with United bodies, supplied in 1928. It was rebuilt as a forward-control bus in 1934, bringing it very much into line with the Lion PLSC range, and survived until 1938. R. L. Wilson Collection

The Tiger TS1 represented an important
stage in the development of single-deck bus
and coach chassis, with its six-cylinder
engine and low build. North Western took 25
of these TS1 in 1929 with rather strange
Leyland 26-seat bodies that looked very
much like double-deckers without the upper
decks. They lasted only until 1931 with North
Western, and most found second homes in
Scotland. Note the 'picture' radiators, which
were a feature of early T range models.
A. Moyes Collection

Coach design improved greatly in the 1930s;
this 1932 Weymann 26-seat body was
mounted on a Yorkshire Woollen Tiger TS1
chassis of 1928 vintage. When
photographed in Nottingham in 1933, it was
operating on the Harrogate-Birmingham
express service.   G. H. F. Atkins

Ribble and Leyland officials display their confidence in the stability of the new breed of double-decker. On the tilt-test at 28 degrees is one of Ribble's 1931 delivery of Titan TD1, with 48-seat lowbridge body. Leyland

Many Titan TD1s enjoyed long and useful lives, like WH 1553, seen here more than 20 years after it was built in 1929, in the fleet of Honeywood of Stanstead. It has since been saved for preservation, and is beautifully restored in its former Bolton Corporation livery by the Lincolnshire Vintage Vehicle Society. Don Morris

Later Leyland bodies on TD1 chassis had enclosed stairs, as shown on this 1929 example for Ortona, Cambridge. At the end of 1929 Ortona was purchased by the LMS and LNE railways, and formed an important part of the new Eastern Counties Omnibus Company when it was formed in 1931. Leyland

Some customers requiring small, normal control chassis received the Badger TA4 goods model, like Wood, Blackpool's FV 1098, seen here after sale to Stark, Dunbar. D. L. G. Hunter

The Tiger TS2 was similar to the TS1, but was intended for bodywork to 26ft, rather than 27ft 6in, length. This was one of six 1930 TS2 supplied to SMT, with Burlingham 27-seat bodywork. Gavin Booth Collection

The three-axle Titanic chassis was considerably less successful than AEC's contemporary Renown. Sheffield Corporation 136, a 1929 TT1, had an impressive 59-seat lowbridge Leyland body. Leyland

Doncaster Corporation 65 was a 1934 Titanic TT2c with Roe 60-seat body, and survived until 1948. Leyland

A four-cylinder Devon General Lion LT1, with functional-looking Hall Lewis 31-seat two-door body, just off the Strand, Torquay, when new in 1930.   Leyland

On test early in 1933, a Lioness LTB1 chassis fitted with a Tangye diesel engine. This was a time of much development work on the diesel engine in road vehicles.
Ian Allan Library

On tour in the early 1930s, a 1929 Lioness LTB1 with Burlingham coach body in the Alexanders fleet. One of two, it was rebodied in 1936, and withdrawn in 1946. Gavin Booth Collection

Loading up at Nottingham in 1935, a Willowbrook-bodied Lion in the Wass Bros fleet, running on hire to Trent. The chassis, new in 1934, was probably a late-model LT5, but features an interim combination of radiator and dumb-irons. G. H. F. Atkins

A smart 1932 Lion LT5 with 32-seat Eastern Counties body in the fleet of the former Tilling & BAT company, Caledonian. Stewart Brown Collection

A neat little Cub KP2 in the Crosville fleet. New in 1933, it was one of eight with Brush 20-seat bus bodies.   Crosville

The driver of a 1932 Cub KP3 in the Alexanders fleet stands proudly by his steed on a private hire. The 20-seat canvas-top body was built by Alexander Motors, of Edinburgh.   Stewart Brown Collection

The Black & White Motorways livery enhances the attractive lines of a 1933 Cub KP3 with 20-seat Duple body.   Duple

Bound for Caernarvon, a Crosville petrol-engined Tiger TS4 of 1933, with a smart Leyland 32-seat rear-entrance coach body. R. L. Wilson Collection

A 1933 petrol-engined Titan TD3 in the Hants & Dorset fleet. Fitted with Brush 52-seat body, it later received a Leyland 8.6 litre oil engine, and in 1937 a Gardner 5LW unit. It is seen in 1949, the year before it was withdrawn, on an inter-dock service at Southampton. Ian Allan Library

Another long-lasting Titan TD3, a 1935
delivery to the fleet of J. Fishwick, of Leyland,
seen in service more than a decade later. It
carries a late example of the original-style of
Leyland 'piano-front' body, which was
replaced by the more modern vee-front
design.   Ian Allan Library

The slimmer radiator shell of the Lion LT5A,
on a 1935 Duple-bodied example for the
London coach fleet of Venture.   Duple

Two Plymouth Corporation Titans illustrate the different radiator styles. At the rear is 128, a 1931 TD1 with Leyland 48-seat lowbridge bodywork; in front is the new 99, a 1935 TD4c with 48-seat Weymann body — note the 'Gearless Bus' wording on the radiator.   Leyland

Under construction at the Brush coachworks at Loughborough in 1936, an East Yorkshire Titan TD4c with petrol engine. The oval plate on the radiator top tank carried the East Yorkshire name; several operators replaced the Leyland name with their own at this time.   G. H. F. Atkins

With an East Kent plate on the radiator, a 1936 Titan TD4 with Brush 56-seat body. It was rebodied in 1948, and lasted in East Kent service until 1962.   Ian Allan Library

Leyland bus chassis have often been used as the basis for goods vehicles, notably as furniture vans. This 1934 Tiger TS6 was used for a more unusual purpose, as the basis of a publicity vehicle for the Daily Mirror. It was used to publicise the 'Daily Mirror 8', a team of girl PT demonstrators, and is seen in Skegness when new. The streamline body was built by Lancefield Coachworks. G. H. F. Atkins

The Tiger TS7 was an extremely popular coach chassis, and most of Leyland's customers took sizeable deliveries. Alexanders received a batch of stylish Alexander-bodied TS7 in 1935, here forming an impressive line-up on private hire work. Many were rebodied as double-deckers during the war — P219 was rebodied in 1943 and lasted until 1960.

The Tigress LTB3 was rare on the home market, although Southdown took six with 20-seat Burlingham coach bodies in 1936. They survived until 1952, and 1823 is seen on an extended tour in Inverness late in its life.

Full-width fronts were popular on coach bodies in the mid-1930s. This Tiger TS7 with rear-entrance Alexander 32-seat body, was one of six delivered to Central SMT in 1936. Robert Grieves Collection

Attractively-proportioned Eastern Coach Works 28-seat bodywork was fitted to this 1937 Tiger TS7 of East Yorkshire. At Nottingham when new. G. H. F. Atkins

In the livery of Imperial Airways, forerunner of BOAC and British Airways, a 1937 Tiger TS7 of Thomas Tilling with Harrington coachwork at Victoria station, London when new. G. H. F. Atkins

A peaceful Victoria Coach Station in 1937, with Tiger TS7s of East Kent and Maidstone & District. The East Kent coaches were new in 1936, with petrol engines, and had Park Royal 32-seat bodies. G. H. F. Atkins

Three-axle Tigers were favoured by operators seeking extra passenger capacity, and Southdown used this 1935 Tiger TS7T on the service from Eastbourne to the top of Beachy Head until it was withdrawn in 1952. The 39-seat centre-entrance was built by Short Bros, and the bus had a petrol engine when new; it received an 8.6litre oil engine in 1940. Michael Dryhurst

The City Coach Company was an enthusiastic user of three-axle Leylands, and built up a fleet of 36 three-axle Tigers between 1935 and 1937. This 1935 TS7T had a Duple body. Ian Allan Library

Central SMT had 19 of these 1935 Tiger TS7Ts with Leyland 39-seat rear-entrance bodies for its busy services around Glasgow. Another bus of the same batch is seen near Llandrindod Wells in 1954, after sale to Ithon Valley. Leyland: R. L. Wilson

The lightweight Cheetah chassis was popular
with SMT group fleets in Scotland; this LZ2A
with 39-seat Alexander coach body was
delivered to Alexanders in 1938 and survived
until 1958. It originally ran in the livery of
Alexander's subsidiary David Lawson, hence
the SN registration.   Don Morris

This 1936 Cub KPZ2 was still in regular
service 28 years later. New to West Riding,
with 24-seat Roe body, it survived with
Pritchard of Newborough, Anglesey, and is
seen in Llangefri in 1962.   A. Moyes

London Transport chose the forward-control SKPZ2 Cub for its eight 1936 Inter-Station coaches. Park Royal built the $1\frac{1}{2}$-deck 18-seat bodies.   London Transport

The 100 London Transport STDs of 1937 were attractive and popular buses. Based on Titan TD4 chassis, they carried Leyland bodywork adapted to London standards. Two are seen at Hendon when new. G. H. F. Atkins

The underfloor-engined Tiger FEC chassis
was developed for London Transport,
becoming its TF class. Most were fitted with
bus bodies, but 12 received 33-seat Park
Royal coach bodies for private hire work.
Only TF9 survived an air raid during the war,
and it seen in postwar days on tour work.
London Transport

Pressed into London Transport relief service
in 1947, a 1938 Tiger TS8 with Harrington
33-seat coach body from the Grey-Green
fleet.   Ian Allan Library

One of the TS8 Specials supplied to Alexanders in 1939/40, with upright driving position to allow maximum space for passengers. The Alexander bodywork seated 39, four more than was normally possible. Similar buses were supplied to the SMT and Western SMT fleets. The bus shown lasted in service for more than 20 years, and was withdrawn in 1963.   Allen T. Smith

Stranded in the Kent snow in 1947, a 1939 Maidstone & District Tiger TS8 with 34-seat rear entrance Eastern Coach Works body. Ian Allan Library

Some operators still specified petrol engines in the immediate prewar period, like Plymouth Co-op, with this 1939 Tiger TS8 with full-fronted Duple 32-seat coachwork. Duple

In 1937 a coach-bodied Gnu was supplied to the Alexanders fleet. The third axle allowed the coach to be built to 30ft overall length, and 40 seats were fitted.   Leyland

1937 also saw the first appearance of the revolutionary Gnu TEP1 which attracted a great deal of interest. Although the engine was mounted at the front, the entrance was ahead of the twin steering axles. The Alexander bus body had seats for 40.
Stewart Brown Collection

The third TEP1 Gnu was built for the City Coach fleet in 1938. It carried attractive Duple 40-seat centre-entrance bodywork. Duple

The ninth of Leyland's experimental twin-steer single-deckers was the single Panda, with horizontal underfloor-mounted engine. Although the chassis was built in 1939, it only entered service in 1941 with Alexanders, with this 45-seat Alexander body. Alexander

Lytham St Annes Corporation favoured full-fronted Leyland bodywork for its Titans. This 1937 TD5c with 54-seat body is seen in service a quarter of a century later.
Stewart Brown

Barton Transport specified stylish forward-entrance Duple bodywork for its 1939 Titan TD5. A few operators favoured this entrance layout in the 1930s, but did not find widespread acceptance until the 1960s.
Duple

The Titan TD6c was only supplied to Birmingham, 85 buses in 1938/39, although many of its improvements appeared on the subsequent TD7. This former Birmingham TD6c with Metro-Cammell body is seen in service with A1, Ardrossan, in the 1950s.

Birmingham City Transport bought 50 Titan TD7c in 1939, and these carried Leyland 52-seat bodies modified to resemble the standard BCT style as supplied by other builders. FOF 296 is seen 23 years later in service with Norfolk's of Nayland.   G. R. Mills

For the notoriously steep Bargoed Hill in South Wales, Leyland supplied the West Monmouthshire Omnibus Board with a modified goods chassis, an Alpine Beaver TSC9 adapted to Bull TQ3 standard. When new in 1935 it had a Weymann body, but in 1944 it received this utility-style Burlingham 32-seat body, as seen in 1959.
Michael Dryhurst

One of 196 'unfrozen' Titan TD7s, assembled in 1941/42 from components in stock. This was one of two built in 1942 for Young's of Paisley, with utility-style Pickering 56-seat bodywork. In 1947 XS 5493 was sold to AA Motor Services, and is seen in 1952 in Ayr.
Don Morris

Leyland

Preserved Leylands

Several hundred Leylands are preserved, a tribute, in many cases, to the exceptionally long lives they have enjoyed in service. One of the oldest is CD 7045, a 1922 G7 with a 1928 Short 51-seat open-top body, now preserved in running order by the Southdown company. It is seen alongside another company-preserved Southdown Leyland, a 1929 Titan TD1 with Brush 51-seat body; open-top bodies were rare by the time the TD1 came along.   Gavin Booth

Restored by the Lincolnshire Vintage Vehicle Society in Lincoln Corporation livery, this 1927 Lion PLSC1 with 31-seat Leyland bodywork was actually new to Blythe & Berwick, of Bradford.   G. R. Mills

An unusual Badger BA4 with passenger
bodywork, supplied in 1930 to Bradford
Education Department with 20-seat Plaxton
body. It is another from the large LVVS
collection of preserved vehicles.
R. L. Wilson

Although preserved in Eastern Counties
livery, this 1929 Titan TD1 came from the
fleet of Southern National. The lowbridge
51-seat Leyland body shows clearly the open
staircase layout of the early Titan bodies.
G. R. Mills

The Leyland 'hybridge' body on early Titans is
well represented by this 1932 Titan TD2
51-seater, originally built for Jersey Motor
Transport. It was one of several elderly
Leylands brought back to the mainland after
long lives in Jersey.   G. R. Mills

The first new buses bought by Sunderland Corporation were 12 1929 Lion LT1 with 32-seat Leyland bodies. Number 2 is now preserved, and is seen at the 1968 HCVC Brighton Rally.   G. R. Mills

A fine view of the front of the 1930 ex-Lancashire United Lion LT1 preserved by the LVVS. It has a 30-seat Roe body, and is seen at a rally at Warwick in 1972. T. W. Moore

The slimmer radiator of the Lion LT5A, on a former Leyland demonstrator which had a Leyland 34-seat rear-entrance body. New in 1934, it was sold in 1935 to Lytham St Annes Corporation, in whose colours it is now preserved.   G. R. Mills

The later Lion LT7c, a 1937 with Leyland 34-seat rear-entrance body, built for Lytham St Annes Corporation. Now preserved, and seen at Brighton in 1967.   G. R. Mills

Now preserved, this 1939 Lion LT8 has Leyland 32-seat front-entrance bodywork, and was new to Eastbourne Corporation, with a petrol engine. It received a diesel engine in 1954.   G. R. Mills

The Leyland Tiger and AEC Regal were
deadly rivals in the 1930s, and they are
contrasted at Harrogate on the Trans-
Pennine Run. The Tiger is a 1937 TS7, one of
22 with Harrington 32-seat rear-entrance
coach bodies. The Regal is a 1931 Craven-
bodied example for Red Bus Service.
Gavin Booth

This ex-Wigan Corporation Titan TD7 was
one of 14 supplied in 1940, with 48-seat
Leyland lowbridge bodywork. At Brighton in
1970.   G. R. Mills

One of the 88 Tiger FEC built for London Transport is now preserved in London Transport's own collection. It has LPTB 34-seat coach bodywork built at Chiswick, and is seen at Stratford-on-Avon in 1970. G. R. Mills

Externally similar, but mechanically very different, is one of London Transport's CR class, rear-engined Cub REC, with LPTB 20-seat bodywork, supplied in 1939/40. G. R. Mills

A familiar entrant at many rallies throughout the country, the ex-Maidstone & District 1937 Tiger TS7 with attractive Harrington 32-seat coach body. G. R. Mills

Roy Marshall's smart ex-Lancashire United 1938 Tiger TS8 with 30-seat Roe bus body, at Battersea in 1972.   G. R. Mills

A few examples of the comparatively rare Comet model are now preserved. This 1950 CPP1, with Harrington 29-seat body, was new to Newton, of Chumleigh.   G. R. Mills

One of many postwar Tigers which are now preserved, a 1948 PS1/1 with 32-seat Park Royal rear-entrance coach body, preserved in the livery of its original owner, Southdown. Gavin Booth

The Northern Ireland Road Transport Board, and its successor, the Ulster Transport Authority, built up a sizeable fleet of Tiger PS1 with NIRTB 34-seat bodies. Among those preserved is this attractive 1947 example. R. C. Ludgate

Ulster Transport Authority was also an enthusiastic Titan operator, and this 1950 PD2/1 with lowbridge UTA 53-seat body (with Leyland-style front and rear ends) was acquired for preservation when it was withdrawn in 1969. R. C. Ludgate

A more recent preserved ex-UTA bus, a 1954 ex-demonstration Tiger Cub PSUC1/5T with Saro 44-seat body. It was withdrawn in 1971, by which time Ulsterbus had replaced UTA. R. C. Ludgate

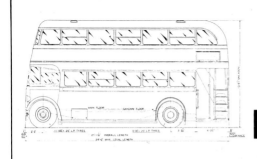

Leyland's 1947 lowbridge body design for the Titan PD2 was clearly derived from the immediate prewar style.

Leyland

Peacetime Reconstruction

Postwar bus production at Leyland commenced late in 1945 with a new double-deck chassis, the Titan PD1, featuring a new 7.4litre engine. The PD1 was joined by its single-deck equivalent, the Tiger PS1, in 1946. From this stage, Leyland distinguished most successive models with a figure suffix, and the wide range of options offered on some models meant that there could be dozens of variations on a particular chassis. So there were PD1/1, PD1/2 and PD1/3 Titans produced — the PD1/3 available for 8ft wide bodies, in line with the relaxation of the maximum legal dimensions.

The PD1 was a valuable stop-gap model, which helped operators re-stock their fleets after the war, but it lacked the sophistication of Leyland's immediate prewar chassis. A bigger-engined model was being developed, and emerged in 1947 as the Titan PD2, with 9.8litre 0.600 engine. The PD2 was produced for more than 20 years, and nearly 40 home variants were produced. During its life the PD2 was available for 7ft 6in or 8ft wide bodies, with vacuum or air brakes, with synchromesh, preselective or pneumo-cyclic (semi-automatic or fully-automatic) gearboxes, or with exposed radiators or full-width grilles. These grilles, were based on a Midland Red design for 100 PD2/12s supplied in 1952/53.

Special PD2s were produced for London Transport from 1948. London had bought 65 virtually standard PD1s in 1946, as a temporary measure, but was attempting to standardise on its RT family, and Leyland supplied 2,131 PD2s with many London features, including 500 8ft wide buses with Leyland bodies.

Leyland's immediate postwar double-deck model was the Titan PD1, which helped satisfy the demand for new buses until the bigger-engined PD2 appeared. This early PD1, for Clyde Coast, carries Leyland bodywork which was virtually identical to the immediate prewar design.

The 0.600 engine was also offered in the Tiger range, the PS2 model introduced in 1948. Its success on the home market was rather preempted by the appearance in 1949 of a production underfloor-engined bus, the Leyland/MCW Olympic, marketed as a complete, integral-construction bus, but British operators preferred the concept of the separate chassis and body, so the Royal Tiger PSU1 joined the range in 1950; both models featured a horizontal version of the 0.600 engine.

The Royal Tiger was a sturdy and powerful chassis, but operators were calling for ways of saving fuel by saving weight, and in 1952 Leyland answered this call with the Tiger Cub PSUC1, with a horizontal 0.350 engine of 5.7litres capacity. The Tiger Cub quickly became successful on the home market, and Leyland and MCW were prompted to have another try at the integral market in 1953, with the Tiger Cub-based Olympian, but with little success.

The 0.350 engine was also offered, from 1952, in an unusual single-deck middleweight chassis, the Comet — a semi-normal control chassis introduced in 1947 with petrol or diesel engine.

While the Tiger Cub was favoured in Britain, successive models of the Olympic and Royal Tiger were built for export customers, including the Royal Tiger Worldmaster, announced in 1954. This chassis, with pneumo-cyclic gearbox and air brakes, could be supplied with a new engine, the 11.1litre 0.680 as an alternative to the 0.600. A few Worldmasters were supplied to home operators where a heavier specification was required, but as an export model it was an outstanding success.

A 1946 Titan PD1 supplied to the Northern Ireland Road Transport Board. The rather severe lowbridge body was by NIRTB. It is seen in 1952, following the formation of the Ulster Transport Authority.   Don Morris

Ribble chose the 8ft wide Titan PD1 3 for its 1948 batch of 'White Lady' coaches. The prototype, with Burlingham 49-seat lowbridge body, is seen in Blackpool bus station when new. Ian Allan Library

Other unusual Titan PD1s were the 10 53-seaters placed in service by Birch Bros in 1946 on its famous 203 London-Rushden service. The unusual forward-entrance bodywork was built by Birch.
Ian Allan Library

An attractive 1948 Tiger PS1 with Duple
32-seat coach body in the Yorkshire Woollen
fleet. It is seen in Derby in 1951.
G. H. F. Atkins

Preston Corporation had two of these 1949
PS1/1s with East Lancs 34-seat rear
entrance bodies; number 75 is seen in
Liverpool in 1962.   R. L. Wilson

Bournemouth Corporation bought three of
the rarer Tiger PS2/1 model, with full-fronted
Burlingham 32-seat coach bodies, in 1949.
All three are now preserved.   Leyland

The bigger OPS3 Tiger range was not supplied to British customers. In Ireland, CIE built up a large fleet, including a number of coaches like this 1951 OPS3/1 with CIE 30-seat body. It is seen in Dublin in 1965.
Michael Fowler

CIE, in Ireland, was a staunch Leyland user for many years. This 1956 Titan OPD2/10 with Leyland-style CIE 66-seat body is shown crossing O'Connell Bridge in Dublin. CIE built bodywork to this design, albeit with the distinctive three-part window at the front of the upper deck, until 1961.
Irish Tourist Board

For many years double-deckers in the East Yorkshire fleet had distinctively-shaped roofs to negotiate the Beverley Bar gateway. Two Titan PD2s with Roe 'Beverley Bar' bodies are seen in 1952 when MKH 82, a PD2/12 with full-fronted coach bodywork, was new; behind is a 1950 PD2/3.   Don Morris

Northern Counties 56-seat bodywork was fitted to this 1949 Titan PD2/1, new to Young's of Paisley, but seen in 1963 in Glasgow in service with Western SMT, who acquired it with the Young's business in 1951.   Michael Fowler

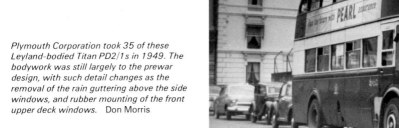

Plymouth Corporation took 35 of these Leyland-bodied Titan PD2/1s in 1949. The bodywork was still largely to the prewar design, with such detail changes as the removal of the rain guttering above the side windows, and rubber mounting of the front upper deck windows.   Don Morris

In Daimler-dominated Birmingham, Leyland managed to sell batches of Titan double-decks. This was one of 100 PD2s with Birmingham-design Brush 54-seat bodies, new in 1948. In New Street in 1966.
T. W. Moore

The lowbridge version of the Leyland body on Titan PD2/3 chassis is represented by this 1950 Ribble example seen in Manchester in 1962.   Michael Fowler

A lowbridge Farington body on Titan PD2/10 chassis, one of 10 supplied to Luton Corporation in 1954, the last year that Leyland bodywork was built.   Leyland

The ultimate Leyland double-deck body style was the Farington design, shown here in Brighton in 1952 on a Southdown Titan PD2/12, one of 24 delivered the previous year.   Ian Allan Library

The 100 Titan PD2/12s built in 1952/3 for Midland Red introduced a new style of full-width front, which was adopted as standard by Leyland. These attractive buses, coded LD8 by their operator, were the only PD2s built new combining this style of front with Leyland Farington bodies.   Don Morris

While many Leyland customers specified the Midland Red-style 'tin front', others remained faithful to the exposed radiator. North Western only had 10 'tin front' Leylands, Titan PD2/21s with Weymann 58-seat lowbridge bodies.   Gavin Booth

Similar lowbridge Weymann bodywork was fitted to nine Titan PD2/22s built for Luton Corporation in 1956.   Leyland

East Midland also operated PD2s with lowbridge Weymann bodies; one of 12 PD2/20s is seen near Bolsover.   Ian Allan Library

The last special bus built for the Bargoed Hill service in South Wales was this 1959 Titan PD2/38 with Willowbrook 31-seat body. When the service was re-routed, avoiding the hill, West Mon had the chassis rebodied as a double-decker.   Gavin Booth

The nationalised Scottish companies were able to buy on the open market, as well as taking Bristol/Eastern Coach Works products. This meant that for some years Western SMT bought lowbridge Leyland Titans as well as lowheight Bristol Lodekkas. This 1955 Titan PD2/20, seen in Glasgow, had Northern Counties 55-seat bodywork.   Leyland

Leyland was proud of its success with the municipal fleets, from the very large Glasgow, Liverpool and Manchester fleets, down to smaller undertakings like Great Yarmouth. At Wellington Pier when new, a 1957 Titan PD2/22, one of five with Massey 58-seat bodies.   Leyland

Newport Corporation specified locally-built Longwell Green bodywork for these 1959 Titan PD2/40s, seen in 1970.   T. W. Moore

Against the fourteenth century twisted spire of the parish church of St Mary and All Saints in Chesterfield, a 1958 Corporation Titan PD2/30 with Weymann 59-seat bodywork; note the extra Leyland badging on the full width front.   Leyland

The partial railway involvement in the Sheffield Joint Omnibus Committee meant that the normally restricted products of Eastern Coach Works could be bought. This resulted in five 1957 Titan PD2/20 for the Sheffield fleet with ECW 59-seat bodies — a combination that remained unique.
Stewart J. Brown

Four attractive East Lancs bodied PD2/20s newly delivered to St Helens Corporation in 1956, in that undertaking's red and cream livery. Ian Allan Library

Glasgow Corporation specified the semi-automatic pneumo-cyclic gearbox from an early stage. This was L24 of 1955, a Titan PD2/25 with 7ft 6in wide Alexander body to Weymann design, loading outside Kelvin Hall; it was destined to be the first of more than 300 PD2s for the Glasgow fleet. Leyland

Edinburgh Corporation bought 300 Titan PD2/20s for tram replacement in 1954-57. They had lightweight Metro-Cammell Orion bodywork with seats for up to 63 passengers. Leyland

Stratford Blue, one of the smaller BET group fleets, bought three of these Titan PD2/12s with Willowbrook 63-seat bodywork in 1956, and 22 is seen when new at Digbeth, Birmingham.   G. H. F. Atkins

Leyland managed to break AEC's monopoly of London Transport supplies with the order for 1,631 Titan PD2/1s — albeit heavily modified — the RTL class. RTL1093 was new in 1950, and had a Park Royal 56-seat body.   Don Morris

London Transport's first 8ft wide motor buses were the 500 RTWs, modified Titan PD2/3s with Leyland 56-seat bodies very much to LT design. The result was most attractive, and RTW137 is seen in 1952 at Victoria.   G. H. F. Atkins

Co-operation with Metro-Cammell produced the integral Olympic model, although few were sold to British operators; most preferred the separate chassis Royal Tiger which followed. Yorkshire Woollen bought ten of these HR44 Olympics in 1951, with 42-seat bodies. G. H. F. Atkins

Following a style set by the AEC Regal IVs for BEA service in London, Manchester Corporation bought six Royal Tiger PSU1/13 in 1953, with distinctive Burlingham bodies featuring a raised passenger area at the rear over an extra-large luggage compartment. Gavin Booth

Although there were other customers for Leyland's unusual coach body on Royal Tiger chassis, it will always be immediately associated with the Ribble fleet, which took 120 examples in 1951. Leyland

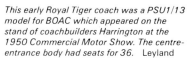

This early Royal Tiger coach was a PSU1/13 model for BOAC which appeared on the stand of coachbuilders Harrington at the 1950 Commercial Motor Show. The centre-entrance body had seats for 36.   Leyland

Leyland offered a bus body for the Royal Tiger, and the most unusual examples were the 16 1952 PSU/9s for Edinburgh Corporation, which retained the traditional Scottish cutaway rear entrance.   Leyland

Leaving Duple's coachworks at Hendon, London for Wales, two Royal Tiger PSU1/13 with 44-seat bodies for the BET group outpost James, of Ammanford. These buses represented the total 1952 deliveries for this small fleet. Duple

While most operators had switched to lighter-weight chassis by 1955, Bolton Corporation opted for this Royal Tiger PSU1/14 with 43-seat East Lancs body. Leyland

The Tiger Cub became very popular in the weight-obsessed 1950s. This PSUC1/1 with Burlingham 44-seat body was new in 1957 to Hill, of Tredegar. Leyland

The BET group fleets were enthusiastic users of Tiger Cubs for bus and coach duties. This 1956 PSUC1/1 with Weymann 44-seat body was one of over 120 supplied to North Western between 1954 and 1960, and is seen in Derby. Leyland

Alexanders built up a large fleet of Tiger Cubs, culminating in batches with Alexander Y-type coach bodies for the Midland fleet. These 1963 PSUC1/2 are seen in Dunkeld. Gavin Booth

Low railway bridges on important routes meant that Edinburgh Corporation required a large single-deck fleet. In 1959-61 Edinburgh bought 100 Tiger Cub PSUC1/3 with Weymann bodies, and 47 is seen in the High Street in 1963. Gavin Booth

The Tiger Cub-based integral Olympian was, like the Olympic before it, a Leyland/MCW collaboration. Few were built, and most were for Western Welsh; six were delivered to Fishwick, of Leyland, in 1957. Michael Fowler

At Monaghan, in Ulster, a Comet CPO1 of the Erne Bus Company.   Michael Dryhurst

Douglas Corporation, on the Isle of Man, bought three of these Comet CPO1 with 30-seat Park Royal bodies in 1949. Number 21 is seen in Douglas in 1964, showing the unusual frontal styling of the Comet chassis. R. L. Wilson

For operators requiring more powerful chassis, the 680-engined Worldmaster was supplied. Glasgow Corporation took 30 Worldmaster RT3/1 in 1956. They had Glasgow Corporation 40-seat two-door bodies on Weymann frames.   Leyland

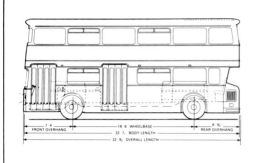

The extra length of the PDR2. 1 Atlantean is shown in this 1968 Park Royal-bodied example for Plymouth Corporation.

Leyland

Bigger and Bigger Buses

As buses got bigger in the 1950s and 1960s Leyland moved ahead with new model ranges which placed them strongly in the forefront of Britain's bus manufacturers. In 1956 30ft double-deckers on two axles were legalised in Britain, and Leyland's initial response was the Titan PD3, a six-model range with options of vacuum or air brakes, synchromesh or pneumo-cyclic gearboxes, exposed radiators or 'tin fronts'. The new length allowed operators to fit bodies with up to 74 seats, and many opted for a forward-mounted entrance. But Leyland's trump card in 1956 was the Atlantean, a new *rear*-engined double-decker.

This was not Leyland's first rear-engined vehicle; there had been the 1936 experimental single-deck and the London Transport Cubs, and in 1952/54 there had been two experimental double-deckers which had small, turbocharged 0.350 engines mounted on the rear platforms. The Atlantean changed all that. The new regulations meant that it could be 30ft long, and the entrance was at the extreme front, ahead of the front axle; the engine was now the 0.600 unit. The MCW body had seats for 78 and was constructed semi-integrally with the underframe, so the Atlantean was initially marketed as a complete bus.

As Leyland and others had found, British operators were reluctant to accept the principle of integral construction, and preferred to mount separate bodies built by their regular suppliers on their chassis. Two years later the Atlantean reappeared in production PDR1/1 form, as a separate chassis, and set the fashion for the standard British double-deck bus of the 1960s and 1970s.

The 1956 Atlantean prototype, in its semi-integral form, was built to the overall height of 13ft 3in; in chassis form it was not possible to produce a low-height bus with normal gangways on both decks, so most Atlanteans were normal height (14ft 6in) buses. Among the early Atlanteans were a number of low-height vehicles which had an unusual upper deck layout, with normal seating at the front, and four rows of four-across seating, with a side gangway, at the rear.

There were other changes to the Leyland bus range at the time. In 1958 the more powerful 0.375 engine was offered in the Tiger Cub, and in 1962 this was succeeded by the 0.400. In 1960 a new-style front-end assembly was offered on the Titan, replacing the Midland Red style of 1952; again this was an operator-inspired design, and became known as the St Helens front. Titans with this front had an extra 'A' in the chassis designation, producing chassis like the PD2A/30 and PD3A/3.

The 1950s had seen a preoccupation with lighter-weight single-deck chassis like the Tiger Cub, but there was a demand for more powerful chassis, and Leyland introduced the Leopard in 1959, designated L1 (bus) and L2 (coach). The Leopard was virtually a Tiger Cub with an 0.600 engine, and proved to be a useful basis for a longer chassis when the British regulations were changed to allow 36ft long buses. New, and very successful, 36ft Leopards, designated PSU3 models, were introduced in 1961, and the L range Leopards were re-designated PSU4 in 1964. More Leopards appeared in 1970, following relaxation of the regulations to allow 39ft 4in buses; these were designated PSU5.

Leyland next turned to rear-engined single-deckers. There had been the export-only Lion model of 1960, an interesting amalgam of Worldmaster and Atlantean, but not a very successful one. More successful, if not wildly so, was the 1964 Panther family. There was the 36ft Panther PSUR chassis, with 600 engine, and its smaller brother the 33ft Panther Cub PSURC, with 400 engine. Both were mainly bought for city bus use, but neither chassis achieved the expected success.

Atlantean chassis were specified by some operators for single-deckers in the 1960s, but the principle of increased standardisation with the double-deck range did not have a wide appeal, and few were built; the Atlantean's main rival, the Daimler Fleetline, was marketed in both single-deck and double-deck forms with rather more success. As a double-decker the attraction of the Fleetline was its low floor line, permitting low-height bodies without the awkward semi-lowbridge layout of the Atlantean; Leyland countered with the PDR1/2 Atlantean in 1964, with the drop centre rear axle of the Albion Lowlander chassis. (The low-floor front-engined Lowlander, built in Glasgow by Albion, was marketed as a 'Leyland' outside Scotland.) The PDR1/2 was not greatly successful, and in 1967 was replaced by the revised PDR1/3. In 1966 a longer Atlantean chassis had appeared, the PDR2.1, suitable for normal-height 33ft bodies.

The Titan had continued to sell alongside the Atlantean, and many operators were sorry to see the withdrawal of the model in 1969. It was notable that the very last Titan, as with many throughout the later life of the model, had a traditional Leyland exposed radiator, in preference to the full-width front end.

The extra length of the Titan PD3 attracted many operators seeking extra passenger capacity, and persuaded many to change to forward entrances. This was one of seven 1958 PD3/5 with Metro-Cammell 72-seat bodies supplied to Preston Corporation, and seen in the drab crimson livery of the time. Leyland

Approaching Nottingham bus station in 1973, a 1961 Titan PD3/6 in the independent South Notts fleet, with lowbridge 64-seat body by Northern Counties.   T. W. Moore

The 'tin front' Titan PD3/3 was popular in Scottish Bus Group fleets, with 67-seat rear entrance bodywork. A 1959 Western SMT example, with Northern Counties body, is seen in Paisley. It features the extra cooling grilles added to the full-width front.
Stewart J. Brown

Southdown was a major Titan PD3 user, all with forward-entrance Northern Counties bodies. These 1964 PD3/4 were convertible open-toppers for summer services on the south coast, and like all Southdown's PD3s, had full-fronted bodies.
Stewart J. Brown Collection

Ulster Transport Authority also specified fully-fronted bodies for its Titan PD3s. This 1961 PD3/4 at Coleraine station had a UTA body built on MCW frames.   Ulsterbus

The 1960 St Helens glass-fibre front had a sculpted look, and was vaguely similar to the front offered on some Leyland goods models. This 1962 Titan PD2A/24 with Weymann 65-seat body was one of four delivered to the Swindon Corporation fleet, a fleet normally dominated by Daimlers.   T. W. Moore

The St Helens front features on this 1967 Bradford Corporation Titan PD3A/2 with East Lancs 70-seat body, seen in 1971. Bradford, which also bought Atlanteans and Fleetlines in 1967, was apparently uncertain about its vehicle requirements. In fact, Bradford bought more PD3s in 1969.   T. W. Moore

The very last PD-series Titan was delivered to Selnec PTE in November 1969, a PD3/14 with East Lancs 73-seat body. It had been ordered by Ramsbottom UDC, which had passed into Selnec PTE, and is seen at Bury in 1977 in the fleet of Greater Manchester PTE, Selnec's successor.   Michael Fowler

Maidstone & District was one of the earliest
Atlantean users; there were 36 of these
PDR1/1 with Metro-Cammell 78-seat bodies
supplied in 1959 to replace Hastings
trolleybuses. The earliest body styles on
Atlantean chassis were rather uneasy, for
designers had still to come to terms with the
rear-engined layout. Leyland

An Atlantean PDR1/1 supplied in 1960 to the
independent fleet of Scout of Preston. The
77-seat body was built by Metro-Cammell,
but was finished by Willowbrook. It is seen in
Preston on the Blackpool-Burnley service.
Leyland

Similar Metro-Cammell bodywork was fitted
to this early Atlantean PDR1/1 retained
within the Leyland group for research and
development work. It spent much of its life as
a proving vehicle for Self-Changing Gears, at
Coventry. T. W. Moore

The bland 'modern' looks of the Atlantean compare with the classic lines of a Leyland-bodied Titan. Both buses in this 1964 view in Derby Market Place were from the Trent fleet, a 1959 Atlantean PDR1/1 with Weymann 73-seat semi-lowbridge bodywork and a 1953 PD2/12 58-seater. The semi-lowbridge body layout involved four rows of bench seats and a side gangway at the rear of the upper saloon.   T. W. Moore

In South Africa, Pretoria built up a fleet of Atlantean PDR1/1 with bodywork built by Bus Bodies (South Africa) Ltd to MCW design.   Stewart J. Brown

The 50 Atlantean PDR1/1 for London Transport in 1965/66 had singularly uninspired 72-seat bodies, built by Park Royal at a time when more attractive designs were available. XA13 is seen in Parliament Square in 1966.   Gavin Booth

Ribble and its subsidiary Standerwick created a sensation with the fleet of Gay Hostess double-deck coaches placed on express services to and from Lancashire. They were Atlantean PDR1/1, with the bigger 680 engine, and the MCW bodies had seats for 50, plus kitchen and toilet accommodation. Three Gay Hostesses, each bound for a different destination, pause at Coventry in 1969.   T. W. Moore

Newcastle quickly became an Atlantean city, with early batches for the Corporation and Northern General group fleets. This 1967 group of Corporation PDR1/1 carry bodies to the improved designs which appeared in the early 1960s. The buses on the right carry Alexander bodies, of the style originally developed for Glasgow Corporation; the other bus carries an MCW body heavily disguised to match the Alexander design, but lacking the subtlety.   T. W. Moore

Atlanteans galore in Bolton bus station. Four of the buses are ex-Bolton Corporation PDR1/1 with East Lancs bodies, in the Selnec PTE fleet when photographed in 1971. Bolton was actively involved in the development of more attractive bodies for rear-engined double-decks. The fifth Atlantean is a Wigan Corporation PDR1/1 with Northern Counties body.   T. W. Moore

Manchester Corporation's Mancunian body of 1968 was a milestone in double-deck design. This was the prototype, 1001, an Atlantean PDR1/1 with Park Royal 73-seat body. Similar vehicles were also supplied on Daimler Fleetline chassis, and there were 33ft Atlanteans and Fleetlines with generally similar bodywork by Park Royal, East Lancs and Metro-Cammell. Leyland

In the unusual dark blue and red livery of
Accrington Corporation, a 1969 Atlantean
PDR1A/1 with East Lancs 78-seat body.
T. W. Moore

Ribble bought 35 Leopard L2 coaches in 1961, fitted with attractive Harrington Cavalier bodies. 1023, seen when new leaving Liverpool on an extended tour to Devon and Cornwall, was a 32-seater, with air suspension.   R. L. Wilson

Midland Red also favoured the short Leopard chassis for coach touring work; this 1966 PSU4/4R with Plaxton 36-seat body is seen in Moffat.   Gavin Booth

An early 36ft Leopard, a PSU3/3RT supplied to Ribble subsidiary Standerwick in 1963, with Plaxton 49-seat body.   R. L. Wilson

All seven Scottish Bus Group fleets bought Leopards, the vast majority with Alexander Y type bodies. This 1973 Eastern Scottish PSU3/3R with 49-seat body is seen in 1974 on the Leicester-Edinburgh service. T. W. Moore

Unusual coach bodywork on Leopard PSU3B/4R chassis — built by East Lancs, a firm not normally associated with coach bodies. It was one of two 49-seaters supplied to Halton Borough in 1975. R. L. Wilson

The important north-east independent, Trimdon Motor Services, built up a sizeable Leopard fleet. This was one of five PSU3E/4R with Plaxton 53-seat bodies, supplied in 1978, and seen in Bishop Auckland.
Michael Fowler

The Alexander M-type body, normally associated with the Scottish Bus Group's motorway coaches, was specified by Ribble in 1972 for this Leopard PSU5/4R. It is seen in 1980 in National Travel (West) ownership. Michael Fowler

An unusual model designed for the Canadian market was the integral Olympic Mk X, with transverse rear engine, and 40ft × 8ft 6in MCW body.   Leyland

Manchester Corporation bought 30 of the Panther PSUR1/1, fitted with Metro-Cammell 44-seat two-door bodies, in 1967.
R. L. Wilson

Manchester also bought 20 of the smaller rear-engined Panther Cub PSURC1/1, with rear-mounted 400 engines. New in 1965, they had Park Royal 43-seat bodies.
R. L. Wilson

Lancaster bought three of these Panther PSUR1/1R in 1967, fitted with East Lancs 53-seat bodywork. Michael Fowler

Sunderland Corporation bought a large number of rear-engined single-deck buses between 1965 and 1974, when the undertaking passed to Tyne & Wear PTE. There were AEC Swifts, Bristol RELLs, Daimler Roadliners, and Leyland Panthers and Panther Cubs; most had bodies of this unusual style. A Panther PSUR1/1, with Strachan 47-seat body, is seen against the Wearmouth Bridge. G. Coxon

In anticipation of Sweden's change from left-hand to right-hand rule of the road, Stockholm Tramways ordered 200 Panther PSUR1/1L with 37ft 6in Park Royal bodies seating 39. Leyland

Coaches on Panther chassis were rare; this was one of 10 PSUR1/2 with Plaxton bodies supplied to Seamarks of Luton in 1968. G. R. Mills

Although single-deck Daimler Fleetlines were fairly common, single-deck Atlanteans were only specified by three operators. Great Yarmouth Corporation bought three PDR1/1 with Marshall 39-seat bodies in 1968. Michael Fowler

Nottingham Corporation developed its own distinctive body shape, here built by Metro-Cammell on Atlantean PDR1/2 chassis. New in 1965, it is seen in 1968. T. W. Moore

The first Atlantean PDR1/2 were supplied to Coventry Corporation — an event as significant to Leyland as a Preston Corporation order for Fleetlines might have been to Daimler. There were 22, delivered in 1964, with Willowbrook 76-seat bodies. T. W. Moore

The market for 33ft double-decks proved to be fairly restricted, with most of the larger fleets opting for shorter vehicles. Bolton Corporation ordered 15 Atlantean PDR2/1 with 86-seat bodies, but they were delivered in 1970 after the Bolton undertaking had been absorbed by Selnec PTE. Gavin Booth

Leyland

Demonstrators

Like most major manufacturers, Leyland maintained a fleet of demonstration buses which allowed operators to evaluate certain models before placing orders. This 1934 Titan TD3c, TJ 3728, proudly proclaiming that it was a 'Gearless Bus' is seen when new on loan to Nottingham Corporation. The Leyland 'vee-front' body is fitted. The bus was sold in 1935 to Preston Corporation. G. H. F. Atkins

This Lion LT2 demonstrator, TF 955, with 35-seat Leyland body, was new in 1930, and in 1931 it was sold to Lawson of Kirkintilloch. It is seen during a trade press test, at Ullswater.   Ian Allan Library

Metro-Cammell built four demonstration Olympics at its Birmingham works in 1949/50, although all subsequent home-market Olympics were built by Weymann, at Addlestone, Surrey. The demonstrators were of the early 27ft 6in long HR40 type, with seats for 40, and KOC 241, seen here, was new in 1950, and sold later that same year to Whittle, of Highley.   MCW

On loan to Manchester Corporation in 1951, MTC 757 was a 1950 Royal Tiger PSU1/13, one of the very first chassis built, with BET-type Brush 44-seat body, one of the very last bus bodies built by Brush.   R. L. Wilson

The sole Titan PD2/15 — with pneumo-cyclic gearbox — was NTF 9, built as a demonstrator in 1951 with Farington-type Leyland 56-seat body. It is seen on loan to Manchester Corporation, and was sold in 1956 to Docherty, Irvine, part of the A1 Service co-operative, which still owned and operated it 30 years after it was built.
P. Sykes

A very early Tiger Cub chassis was fitted with Saro 44-seat bodywork, and became demonstrator OTC 738, new in 1952. It is shown in service with Ribble in Preston; Ribble went on to build up a sizeable fleet of Tiger Cubs.   R. L. Wilson

A similar Tiger Cub demonstrator, but a PSUC1/3 with pneumo-cyclic gearbox, was built in 1952, and spent some time in London Transport service. After completing its career as a demonstrator, PTE 592 was transferred to the Leyland Motors Social & Athletic Club, as seen here in 1958.   R. L. Wilson

Saunders-Roe also built the bodywork on STF 90, the 1953 PDR1 Lowloader, with rear-mounted engine. It was sold by Leyland in 1957, and by 1961 had found its way into the fleets of Strowgers, of Manchester; it was sold for scrap in 1963. Michael Fowler

The second PDR1 prototype was XTC 684, built in 1954 with Metro-Cammell 61-seat bodywork. It lacked the trolleybus-style full front of STF 90, but had a front styling reminiscent of the experimental London Leyland single-decks of the 1930s. Like STF 90 it was sold in 1957 to Lowland Motorways, of Glasgow, but then passed to Buckmaster, of Leighton Buzzard. It has since been preserved. G. R. Mills

The introduction of the production Atlantean PDR1/1 produced a veritable rush of Leyland demonstrators. The first was the widely-travelled 398 JTB, with standard Metro-Cammell 78-seat bodywork. Painted in Maidstone & District-style green and cream, it is seen in 1960, on loan to Birkenhead Corporation. In 1961 it was sold to Scout, of Preston. R. L. Wilson

The low-height Atlantean PDR1/1 demonstrator was 661 KTJ of 1959, with MCW 73-seat body, seen here undergoing braking tests on a trade press road test. It was sold in 1960 to Bamber Bridge Motor Services, and passed to Ribble with that company in 1967. Ian Allan Library

A later Atlantean demonstrator was KTD 551C of 1965, a PDR1/1 with 680 engine and Sheffield-style Park Royal 74-seat body. It is seen in Glasgow, on loan to Western SMT, which never operated any Atlanteans; in fact, none of the Scottish Bus Group fleets bought new Atlanteans, preferring the Daimler Fleetline. Gavin Booth

Two Leyland Group demonstrators in the Demonstration Park outside the 1966 Commercial Motor Show at Earls Court. On the left is an Albion Viking VK43L with the rare Park Royal Royalist coach body; alongside is YTB 771D, a new Panther Cub PSURC1/1 with Strachan 43-seat body — complete with the inevitable '007' route number. This was sold in 1968 to Eastbourne Corporation.   Gavin Booth

The last Atlantean demonstrator was MTF 665G, a 1968 PDR2/1 with Park Royal 79-seat two-door body, seen here outside Earls Court when new. It was sold in 1971 to Docherty, of Irvine, part of the A1 Service co-operative.   Gavin Booth

In 1973, Leyland National built RRM 148M, the Surburban Express demonstrator. This had a flat saloon floor, with all seats facing forward. It is seen in Linlithgow on loan to Alexanders (Midland); at that time, the Scottish Bus Group had not ordered any Nationals.   Gavin Booth

Demonstrators contrasted in 1978. The second PDR1 prototype XTC 684, with MCW body, alongside Titan prototype 05, registered BCK 706R.   Stewart J. Brown

BCK 706R was the first B15 to carry the Titan name, and appeared with this in 1977. Finished in London Transport livery, it was used in LT service during 1978.   Leyland

The first of Leyland's B15 prototypes to enter service was 04, which as NHG 732P was used by London Transport between 1976 and 1978. It was later painted blue and grey for wider demonstration work, and is seen in 1978 on loan to South Yorkshire PTE. Michael Fowler

A more unusual demonstrator was this unregistered left-hand drive Leyland DAB articulated bus which was tried on airside services by British Airways in 1980. Leyland

The local independent bus operator based in Leyland, J. Fishwick, has provided several buses from its own Leyland National fleet for temporary use as demonstrators. This National 2 demonstrator visited several fleets in 1980/81, and WRN 413V is seen on loan to Colchester Borough. G. R. Mills

The Titan reborn — Leyland's sophisticated double-deck model for the 1980s.

Expansion brings Problems

After many years as a well-respected Lancashire-based bus and truck manufacturer, Leyland started to expand its empire. It now transpires that Leyland had been active in many schemes, over a long period, in promoting mergers between principal commercial vehicle builders in Britain, but apart from the acquisition of Albion Motors in 1951, it was 1961 before the first of a series of take-overs changed the whole shape and direction of the Leyland business — and, ultimately, of the whole British motor industry. The purchase of the Standard-Triumph car business in 1961 was a significant move, but the real coup was the AEC take-over in 1962. AEC had long been Leyland's most obvious competitor, and its arrival in the Leyland fold brought with it the Park Royal and Roe coachbuilding firms.

The growing size of Leyland was reflected in the creation of the Leyland Motor Corporation in 1963, and in 1967 the Rover car business was added to the take-over list. On the bus side LMC bought shares in Bristol and Eastern Coach Works, nationalised since 1948, and reciprocated by selling the Government a share in Park Royal and Roe.

But 1968 was the real turning-point, when Leyland concluded protracted negotiations to acquire British Motor Holdings, the combine which had merged BMC with the Jaguar group. Leyland's importance was reflected in the title British Leyland Motor Corporation, and on the bus front Leyland now found itself in control of virtually all its one-time competition — notably AEC, Bristol, Daimler and Guy.

The end of the 1960s was a traumatic time for the bus industry. Not only was the new BLMC giant trying to find its corporate feet, but there was also the new Transport Act of 1968 which, among other things, introduced a system of Bus Grants to help operators buy buses suitable for one-man operation. Added to this, the former Tilling and BET groups were combined as the National Bus Company in January 1969, and from the end of that year the new concept of Passenger Transport Authorities and Executives was introduced, combining the corporation fleets in four of the largest conurbations; at a stroke, 20 good Leyland group customers were reduced to four. But since Leyland had a virtual monopoly of the heavy end of the bus market, there was no immediate cause for alarm.

BLMC found itself with a proliferation of duplicating bus models, and set about pruning the range. Among the Leyland Motors models which disappeared were the Titan and Tiger Cub, but there were important new models to come. Most significant was the Leyland National, unveiled in 1970, a highly-standardised integral city bus; the fruits of a liaison between Leyland and National Bus, the new bus was designed to be assembled at a new plant at Workington. The rear-engined National was available in 10.3m or 11.3m forms, with one or two doors, and with left or right-hand drive. It had a turbocharged Leyland 510 engine, air suspension and a generally advanced specification. The body — Leyland's return to bodybuilding after 16 years — departed from contemporary thoughts on styling, with its distinctive roof-mounted pod at the rear, housing the heating and ventilating equipment. The National was designed for volume production, and around 1,000 were built each year, sounding the death-knell for Leyland's Panther family, and other adopted models.

In 1972 the Atlantean specification underwent a major updating, and the AN68 range replaced the PDR models. There were two models, AN68.1R for 9.5m bodies, and the longer-wheelbase AN68.2R for 10m bodies. A further rear-engined double-decker was produced at Leyland from 1973, when production of the Daimler Fleetline was switched from Coventry; from the 1976 the Fleetline was sold under the 'Leyland' name.

Leyland double-decks were now facing competition from other builders, who stepped in at a difficult time. Leyland was encountering criticisms from operators, unhappy with the company's monopoly of the double-deck market; and the industrial difficulties of 1973/74 meant that chassis production had slipped badly behind. Leyland's answer was project B15, an advanced integral double-decker with air suspension, power hydraulic brakes and a rear-mounted engine. The body, with its distinctive deep lower deck windows, was designed with great emphasis on passenger and driver requirements.

The B15 was launched as Titan in 1977, and while the original intention was to produce the bus at Park Royal's coachworks in London and then at the AEC Southall works, the AEC plan was dropped, and production commenced at Park Royal in 1978. Industrial relations problems at Park Royal led to the closure of the coachworks in 1980, and transfer of Titan production to Workington. The sophistication of the Titan meant that it has found a specialised market, aimed as it was at London Transport and the PTE fleets. For the other operators, requiring bodies from their normal suppliers, or low-height bodies, a separate chassis was evolved and launched in 1980 as the Leyland Olympian. The Olympian is built at Bristol, and was designed from the outset to replace the Fleetline, Bristol VRT and, ultimately, Atlantean.

The single-deck range was updated in 1979 with the appearance of

Plymouth City bought a large fleet of Leyland Nationals between 1972 and 1974. Two 1151/2R models, 11.3 metre 46-seaters, are seen in 1974. T. W. Moore

the National 2, which featured the bigger 680-series engine in response to operators requests; the body style was largely unchanged, except for a more bulbous front end to incorporate the front-mounted radiator. This added to the length of the National, and basic models were offered in 10.6m and 11.6m versions.

The long-established Leopard was still selling well through the 1970s, but it was showing its age, particularly when considered with its opposition in the heavyweight coach class. The result was the B43 project, first shown to operators in 1980, with front-mounted radiator, air suspension and turbocharged underfloor-mounted engine. It went into production in 1981 as the Tiger, reflecting Leyland's welcome decision to re-use respected type names. Following the reappearance of the Titan, Leyland has produced not only the Tiger and Olympian, but also the Cub — the name given to a midi-size front-engined chassis built at Bathgate — and the Lion, the chassis version of the National, intended primarily for those markets with a requirement for locally-built bodywork.

With the gradual disappearance of the models designed by the companies which passed into Leyland's hands, more and more of the bus range carried the Leyland name. Indeed, several other models were given the 'Leyland' name later in their lives — sometimes a trifle uneasily; in addition to Leyland Fleetlines, there have been Leyland Vikings, which were really Albions, and Leyland Victorys, which were really Guys. But after more than 70 years in use, the Leyland name is still a proud one in the world commercial market — particularly after British Leyland decided to underplay the Leyland name on its cars, hence BL Cars, and emphasise tradition by naming its bus and truck division Leyland Vehicles Ltd. The name now has less geographical significance, for Leyland buses are built in Bristol (Lion and Olympian), Workington (National and Titan), Bathgate (Cub) — and Leyland (Tiger).

The familiar lines of the integral National, with its roof-mounted pod, on a 1975 11351/1R with one-door 49-seat body. T. W. Moore

The shorter-length 10.3 metre National was distinguished by the shorter side windows — although to match the wider door, the fourth passenger window is from the longer National. This Portsmouth 10351/2R with 38 seats was new in 1976. Michael Fowler

London Country has built up a massive fleet of Nationals, including a number of dual-purpose seated versions, which were originally used on Green Line service. This 1976 10351/1R has a 39-seat body.
Stewart J. Brown

One of Leyland's variations on the National theme was the Super National Business Commuter, a mobile office-cum-boardroom filled with electronic gadgetry. Seen in 1978 at the Royal Showground at Stoneleigh.
T. W. Moore

The economy B series version of the 10.3m National introduced a podless roof line, clearly shown here on a Crosville 10351B/1R 44-seater on an Aberystwyth local service.
A. Moyes

The improved AN68/1R Atlantean, one of many in the West Yorkshire PTE fleet, wearing the unusually-applied green and cream livery of the time. The 76-seat Roe body demonstrates the PTE's variant of the standard body style favoured by many operators. It is seen in Leeds in 1975. T. E. Sutch

Few double-deck buses are sold new to non-psv operators; in 1975 Hale Trent Cakes bought this Atlantean AN68/1R with East Lancs body for transporting employees to and from work. No destination gear was fitted, allowing three extra seats to be situated on the upper deck.   Leyland

In Ireland, CIE's last batch of Atlanteans were AN68/1R models with Irish-built bodies by Van Hool-McArdle to this rather square design. This was the 1974 prototype.
Ian Allan Library

Although Van Hool-McArdle bodies were built for British operators on Volvo Ailsa chassis, only one body was mounted on Atlantean. This was for South Yorkshire PTE, and carried the unusual body style introduced for its Ailsas. A 1976 AN68A/1R with 70 seats, it is seen in Sheffield in 1977.
Michael Fowler

In 1973, OK Motor Services of Bishop Auckland bought three of these attractive Atlantean AN68/2R with Northern Counties 83-seat bodies.   Stewart J. Brown

AN68 Atlanteans were supplied to several important export customers, including New York, Singapore, Tehran, Baghdad, Kuwait and Manila. This was one of 400 AN68/2Ls with Park Royal 86-seat bodies for Baghdad Passenger Transport Service.   Leyland

Although the Titan did not turn out to look quite as dramatically different as the project B15 artist's impression suggested, the deep 'standee' lower-deck windows certainly gave it a unique appearance. The first three of London Transport's intitial order for Titans parade in Parliament Square in 1978. They were built at Park Royal, with 69-seat bodies, and are designated TNLXB2RRSp. Leyland

The only municipal customer for the first production run of Titans was Reading Transport, which took two TNLXB2RRSp models in 1979. Leyland

For South Yorkshire PTE, Leyland drew on the resources of several of its factories. The chassis of the five articulated buses supplied in 1980 were built in Denmark by DAB, a Leyland subsidiary, and the body was assembled from standard National parts at Workington. Stewart J. Brown

Two of the first production Olympians on the test-track at Leyland. Both carry lowheight ECW bodies based on the Titan design, but with equal-depth windows on both decks. The bus on the left, with a Bristol VRT-style grille, was used for proving by Leyland, while the bus in Ribble livery carries the standard front end. It was placed in experimental service in 1980.   Leyland

Another prototype Olympian ONTL11/1R was exhibited at the 1980 Motor Show in Strathclyde PTE livery. It carried the prototype Alexander R-type body, with seats for 76.   Alexander

A further prototype Olympian, an ONLXB/1R, was destined for evaluation work in Scotland. With ECW 77-seat body, it was first used on comparison tests in 1981 with Alexanders (Midland) in Glasgow.   SBG

The prominent nose of the National 2, with its front-mounted radiator. This view of a 1980 Merseyside PTE delivery, shows the extra length of the 11.6m version. At Woodside Ferry, Birkenhead, this is a 49-seat NL116L11/1R model. R. L. Wilson

With the introduction of the National 2, the basic specification, without pod, became available on both 10.6m and 11.6m variations. This 1980 East Midland delivery, seen at Chesterfield, is a 49-seat NL116L11/1R model. Michael Fowler

A comparison of National front ends on the Runcorn Busway. Both are Halton Borough vehicles; 26 a 1980 NL116L11/1R, and 24 a 1979 11351A/1R. Michael Fowler

The Leopard continued to sell well to coach customers, mainly in 11m and 12m form. This 1980 National Travel (East) delivery is a PSU5C/4R with 12m Duple Dominant II 53-seat body.   Michael Fowler

Duple Dominant II bodywork is also fitted to this 1979 11m Leopard PSU3E/4R for Crosville, and wearing the special Town Lynx livery for the Flint-Manchester express service.   R. L. Wilson

Premier Travel, the famous Cambridge independent bus and coach operator, and a former AEC Reliance customer took delivery of ten Leopard PSU3F/4R in 1979, fitted with Plaxton Supreme Express bodywork. Seen in Cambridge when new.   Leyland

The first of the new breed of Bathgate-built Leyland Cub, the 1979 prototype model with 29-seat Wadham Stringer Vanguard body.
Wadham Stringer

Following experimental operation of a Leyland DAB articulated bus on airside duties at London's Heathrow Airport, British Airways bought seven of these artics in 1981, with bodies incorporating National units; the buses were assembled by Roe in Leeds.   Leyland

The first examples of Leyland's new Tiger coach were launched in 1981. Two of the prototypes, both TRCTL11/3R models, are seen in Morocco, a Van Hool– bodied demonstrator, and a Duple Dominant III-bodied coach for Eastern Scottish Scotland-London services. The chassis (left) shows the front-mounted radiator, mid-mounted engine and air suspension. A welcome feature on the Tiger was the reintroduction of picture badging (below), and a Leyland Bus logo which echoed the traditional Leyland Motors lettering.   Leyland

Leyland

Rebuilt and Rebodied

Many Leylands over the years have been rebodied — or more drastically rebuilt — for further service. This 1934 Titan TD3 in the Yorkshire Woollen fleet was already 14 years old when rebodied by Roe in 1948. It is seen in Leeds in 1955 with its second body; it lasted in this form until 1959.
G. H. F. Atkins

Many of the SMT group's large fleet of Leylands were rebodied during and after the war, like this 1936 Titan TD4 of Western SMT, seen leaving Kilmarnock bus station with its 1950 Northern Counties 53-seat lowbridge body. It was withdrawn in 1960 — for further service.   Allen T. Smith

The Beadle coachbuilding firm undertook much rebuilding work in the early postwar years. This chassisless Crosville Leyland/ Beadle 35-seat rear-entrance bus, seen in 1953, was one of 20 rebuilt from 1937 Cubs in 1949/50. The fully-fronted bodies incorporated the original radiators. R. L. Wilson

More familiar Beadle rebuilds were the chassisless full-fronted coaches, like this 1952 East Kent example, seen on the South Coast Express service, at Brighton in 1953. The running units were new in 1938 on a Titan TD5 double-decker.   Michael Dryhurst

Leyland bodies were rarely specified for rebodying; in fact, only eight Leyland bodies were built after the war on older chassis, for Plymouth Corporation. This is one of the eight 1938 Titan TD5c, with its 1953 53-seat lowbridge Farington-type body. It is now preserved.   G. R. Mills

Preston Corporation undertook some remarkable rebuilding of all-Leyland Titan PD2/10s between 1961-65. They were lengthened to 30ft, the entrances and stairs were moved to the front, and four, which had started life as lowbridge buses, were 'heightened' to normal height. Number 10, shown here, was new in 1954 with a lowbridge body, and is seen after its 1962 rebuilding.   P. Sykes

Barton Transport assembled a varied selection of Leyland chassis, and rebuilt and rebodied them to produce what the company classed its BTS type. This 1951 BTS1, with Barton 43-seat body, shows the ornate styling carried by many of these useful vehicles.   Michael Fowler

One of the most bizarre rebuildings carried out in recent times was Northern General's conversion of what had been a standard 1958 Titan PD3/4. The driver's cab and controls were moved back behind the front axle and engine, creating what was in effect a normal-control double-decker, to permit one-man operation. The Metro-Cammell body was modified to forward entrance layout, seating 68 passengers, and the engine and radiator were concealed behind a Routemaster-style front. The whole bus was re-registered, numbered 3000, and named 'Tynesider'.   Gavin Booth

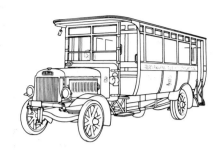

Leyland Bodywork

1919 Leyland bodywork on G chassis for Birkenhead Corporation.

No other British bus chassis builder has been so closely involved in the concept of complete buses as has Leyland over the years. From the earliest days, Leyland offered charabanc and saloon bodywork for its chassis. After World War 1 a new range of styles was evolved for the normal and forward control models of the time, well-built bodies with simple, square lines.

A distinctively Leyland design emerged with the introduction of the L range in 1925, bodies with a pronounced roof dome — the style particularly associated with the PLSC Lion models.

Although double-deck bodies had been built, the Leyland body for the Titan in 1927 set new standards. Suddenly, other designs of the same era appeared outmoded by comparison. The original Titan was a lowbridge design with an open rear staircase; before long, highbridge and enclosed staircase models were available. Identical bodies were produced by other builders for Titan chassis, under contract.

The contemporary single-deck Leyland bodies on Lion and Tiger chassis looked rather like cut-down double-deckers, but in 1931 a more stylish design, with arched tops to the side windows, was introduced. With the spread of long-distance coaching in the 1930s, more attention was paid to the styling of single-deck bodies, and attractive designs were produced for the TS6 Tigers, for example.

All-metal Leyland bodies were introduced in 1934, in place of the traditional composite (wood and metal) construction. A new double-deck body, with distinctive vee front, was introduced that year on the TD3 Titan, and the following year a most attractive new single-deck body was offered on current Tiger and Lion models.

The double-deck style was changed in 1936, with the introduction of a new five-bay body, widely regarded as a pace-setting classic. London Transport took a variation of this body on its 100 Titan TD4s in 1937. Similar adaptations of the Leyland design were later produced for Manchester and Birmingham Corporations, in the days when many of the largest fleets had their own distinctive body styles. The basic Leyland double-deck body was further developed, and improved, with a rounded rear dome in 1939.

By this time Leyland was concentrating on double-deck bodies, and very few single-decks emerged from the bodyshops in the last peacetime years before the outbreak of war led to the cessation of bus production.

When Leyland resumed bus building after the war, it concentrated on double-deck bodies for its new PD1 and PD2 Titans. The body differed little from the 1939 design, and was also produced by Alexander, to help production. No single-deck body was offered for the contemporary Tiger PS1 and PS2 models, and when the integral Olympic appeared, the bodywork was built by Metropolitan-Cammell Weymann. This did not signify an end to Leyland single-deck body production, however, and coach and bus bodies were offered for the Royal Tiger chassis from 1950/51.

The most non-standard postwar bodies were 500 produced to London Transport design on PD2/3 Titan chassis — the RTW class. The final version of the 1939 double-deck body appeared in 1950, with the Farington style, and the last Leyland body produced, in 1954, was to this handsome design. Leyland had decided to close the bus bodyshop and concentrate on chassis production.

Since that time, Leyland has worked closely with several bodybuilders, notably MCW, to produce integral buses, but it took the appearance of the Leyland National in 1970 to mark Leyland's own return to bodybuilding. The Titan double-deck is another example where the bodywork is strictly 'Leyland', particularly following the move to Workington.

Leyland's own bodywork was specified by many operators from the earliest days of the company. This Edinburgh-style 32-seat body was fitted to this 1919 G-type for Birkenhead Corporation. At a time when bodywork was still fairly anonymous, Leyland had already developed a recognisable style.   Leyland

The prototype Titan TD1 had lowbridge Leyland 51-seat bodywork, introducing the 'piano-front' style, with a rear open staircase. It was a clear advance on contemporary body styling, and was widely copied.   Leyland

The 'hybridge' Leyland body style developed the 1927 design in a logical and attractive fashion, with enclosed stairs. This 1931 Titan TD1 was one of three built for the United fleet. Leyland

This style of Leyland single-deck body was offered in the 1930-32 period, and marked a welcome step towards more rounded, more stylish designs. This 1932 Tiger TS4 was delivered to H. M. S. Catherwood Ltd, of Belfast. Leyland

The attractive big-windowed Leyland coach body that was supplied on Tiger TS6 to Ribble and East Yorkshire, and to Leah Bros, of Huthwaite, Nottinghamshire on this 1934 example. G. H. F. Atkins

The all-metal vee-front body that was introduced for double-deck Leylands in 1934, shown here on a Titan TD4 for the fleet of Ledgard, of Leeds.   Leyland

One of the most attractive Leyland bus body styles of the 1930s was this smooth-looking design, complete with radiused window tops, as shown on a 1935 Lion LT7c 35-seater for Preston Corporation.   Leyland

Similar bodywork, but with front entrances, was fitted to 15 Tiger TS7c built for West Riding in 1936; one is seen in 1936 in Barnsley.   G. H. F. Atkins

The 1936 Leyland double-deck body had classic lines and excellent proportions. This was a lowbridge body for Central SMT, one of 15 53-seaters built in 1937 on Titan TD4 chassis. Leyland

The improved version of the 1936 double-deck body was introduced in 1939, the most noticeable change being the radiused rear dome. This 1939 Titan TD5, again for Central SMT, permits comparison. Leyland

Leyland-built coach bodies were always relatively rare, and this was an example of the extremely uncommon immediate prewar design. The vehicle itself is something of a mystery. Delivered to Lincolnshire in 1940, it appears to be a Tiger, although the radiator is non-standard, suggesting a development which would have been announced but for the war. The body had seats for 35, and this unusual coach is seen at Newark in 1940. G. H. F. Atkins

Postwar bodybuilding resumed at Leyland with designs which were very little different to the 1939 body. This 1949 Titan PD2/1 for East Midland had 53-seat bodywork.
Leyland

The timeless lines of the 1936 double-deck Leyland body looked equally appropriate on the postwar Titan PD2/3 chassis — this bus was delivered to Yorkshire Woollen in 1949, and is seen in Dewsbury in 1950. The provision of multiple half-drop windows suggests that this bus was originally built for an export customer. G. H. F. Atkins

The ultimate development of the 1936 body was the Farington design, regarded by many as a classic. The improved glazing gave the design a greater feeling of solidity, and Leyland's decision to stop building bus bodies brought this style to a premature end. This 1953 Titan PD2/12 for West Riding, seen in 1954 in Wakefield, had a 53-seat lowbridge body.   G. H. F. Atkins

Leyland's body design for the Royal Tiger chassis was square, and fairly simple, like many of its contemporaries, but had an unusually shallow roof line. This Trent Royal Tiger PSU1/7, was one of ten 44-seaters delivered in 1952.   Leyland

The Leyland coach body for Royal Tiger, while similar in many respects to the bus design, was notably different from other coach bodies of the time, with its distinctive front windscreen arrangement. This 1952

Royal Tiger PSU1/15, with 41-seat centre-entrance body, is seen on the Doncaster-Wakefield route of Bingley, of Hemsworth, part of United Services.   Leyland

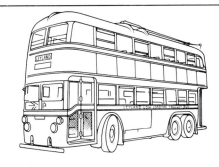

Trolleybuses

The unique low-loading TTL trolleybus of 1935, with Massey bodywork.

Many of the major bus builders became involved in trolleybus manufacture during the 1920s, and like rivals AEC, Daimler and Guy, Leyland widened its horizons by building small batches of trolleybuses from 1928. The first Leyland trolleybuses, for municipal customers like Bradford and Birmingham, were based on contemporary Lion and Titan chassis, but in 1932 the custom-built TB range was introduced. There was the two-axle TB chassis, and the three-axle TTB chassis, and like the contemporary motor bus models, specifications were constantly updated, and model numbers changed accordingly.

Leyland trolleybuses sold steadily to home and overseas customers, but never in anything like the quantities of its motor bus models. But, as with the motor bus models, the prize was London Transport business, for the recently-formed LPTB was building up its large trolleybus fleet in the 1930s, and orders were fairly evenly divided between AEC and Leyland for the supply of around 1,700 trolleybuses in the 1935-41 period.

An elderly-looking Leyland trolleybus at Atherton. It was a 1937 TTB4 model with Roe 64-seat body in the fleet of South Lancashire Transport. It is seen in 1958, the year the bus was withdrawn, and, in fact, the year SLT trolleybuses disappeared, to be replaced by Lancashire United buses.
Michael Dryhurst

Leyland's contributions were mainly TTB4 chassis, dubbed LPTB 70. More than half had Leyland-built bodies.

By 1940, when war brought production to a stop, Leyland had built more than 1,400 trolleybus chassis, and more than 60% were for London use. Most had been conventional two and three-axle chassis, but there was an experimental chassisless vehicle and twin-steer prototype, both of which entered London service, and the advanced low-loading TTL model, which was built in 1935.

After the war Leyland continued to build trolleybuses, but not under its own name. In an unusual alliance between arch-rivals, Leyland and AEC formed British United Traction, and from 1946 until 1965 built and sold trolleybuses under the BUT name. In general, Leyland's models were for export and AEC's for the domestic market.

Leyland built its first BUT trolleybuses at the Kingston-upon-Thames factory, but in 1948 production transferred to Leyland. The only Leyland-built BUTs for British customers were built for Glasgow Corporation in 1950/53 and 1958. These were RETB/1s, for Leyland and AEC each continued to use characteristic type designations.

A newer-looking Roe 64-seat body on a 1938 TTB4 model. Like several 'SLT' trolleybuses, it was actually owned by Bolton Corporation, but was operated by SLT in SLT livery. It lasted in service until 1958.
Michael Dryhurst

London Transport was a major customer for Leyland trolleybuses, and this was one of its F1 class, 100 TTB4 with Metro-Cammell 70-seat bodies delivered in 1937. At Shepherds Bush in 1960.   Michael Dryhurst

Manchester Corporation first operated trolleybuses in 1938, and among its first deliveries was this TTB4 with Crossley/MCW 68-seat body to Manchester's famous streamline style. It is seen in 1954, and was withdrawn two years later.   R. L. Wilson

Following the amalgamation of Leyland and AEC trolleybus interests to create British United Traction in 1946, AEC developed home-market chassis and Leyland export models. The only exceptions were special Leyland-built vehicles supplied to Glasgow Corporation, using export-type chassis. The first was this RETB1, fitted with Weymann 26-seat Standee body, built in 1950. Early in 1951 it was demonstrated to operators over the South Lancashire system (the nearest to Leyland), and Glasgow TB35 is seen in Atherton. Ten similar buses followed in 1953. Leyland

Glasgow Corporation was given special permission to operate a batch of single-deck trolleybuses which were longer than the 30ft permitted at the time. There were ten BUT RETB1, built in 1958, with Burlingham 50-seat bodies built to 34ft 5½in overall length. Their successful operation led to the relaxation of dimensions to allow 36ft buses in 1961. Leyland

Tailpiece

The original style of lowbridge Leyland bodywork on Titan TD1 had a distinctive outside staircase leading to the offside sunken gangway. This 1928 Sheffield Corporation TD1 had been acquired by Alexanders when seen in 1935.
Gavin Booth Collection